Time-Savers for Teachers

GRAMMAR YEARS 3-4

Peter Clutterbuck

W

FRANKLIN WATTS

LONDON·SYDNEY

How to use this book

This book provides a range of worksheets suitable for children in Years 3 and 4 of primary school. The worksheets are grouped into sections that correspond to the sentence level work specified in the National Literacy Strategy. The contents are equally relevant to the Scottish 5-14 Guidelines, and the curricula for the Republic and Northern Ireland.

Each section starts with an *introduction* that sets the topic in context. The worksheets that follow are mostly laid out in pairs, with the left- and right-hand pages catering for *different* levels of ability. Complete *answers* are provided to save time with marking. You can then keep the worksheets as part of the pupils' *assessment* records.

All teacher-pages have a vertical stripe down the side of the page. All the worksheets are photocopiable.

This edition first published in 2004

Franklin Watts
338 Euston Road, London NW1 3BH

UK adaptation by Brenda Stones
Educational advisers: Sarah St John, Jo Owston

This edition not for sale outside the United Kingdom and Eire

ISBN 978 0 7496 5799 4

Printed in Dubai

Franklin Watts is a division of Hachette Children's Books.

Contents

Grammatical awareness

Contents

Sentence construction and punctuation

Introduction to Nouns

National Literacy Strategy objectives

From the beginning of Key Stage 2, the National Literacy Strategy begins to use the terminology of word classes more deliberately: so in Year 3 specific mention is made of collective nouns, plural forms of nouns, and proper nouns:

Y3T2 S4: understanding the term 'collective noun' and collecting examples – experiment with inventing other collective nouns;

Y3T2 S4: noticing which nouns can be pluralized and which cannot, e.g. trousers, rain;

Y3T2 S8: other uses of capitalisation from reading, e.g. names.

Introducing nouns

Before starting on the worksheets, teachers will want to revise the concept of nouns as 'naming words'.

You could brainstorm a list of common nouns for each letter of the alphabet, as a form of I-spy around the classroom.

Then remind pupils of the role of proper nouns, i.e. the use of capital letters for names, places and days of the week.

Introduce the idea of collective nouns, and the benefits of classifying or grouping sets of objects.

On plural forms, first remind pupils of the regular plural as 's' and the irregular plurals for children, men, women etc. Then teach the rules for plural 'es' after ch, sh, s; 'ies' after consonant and y, and 'ves' after f and fe.

Class activities

Help children to cut out a large shape from paper, for example a bird shape. Children then write the names of things that belong in that shape. The name shapes can then be displayed around the classroom.

After discussing common collective nouns with children (a flock of birds, a herd of cattle) ask them to make up some new ones of their own. Suggest a couple to start them off such as a slither of snakes or a hop of frogs.

Worksheet answers

Answers are provided on page 12.

From Time-Savers for Teachers: Grammar Years 3-4. This page may be reproduced for classroom use.

5

Proper Nouns

Name _____

Proper nouns are the names of particular people, places or things. They are written with a capital letter at the beginning.

1. Add a word from the box to complete each sentence.

> days   students   months   planets   cities   countries

a. England, Vietnam and China are all _____ .

b. Monday, Sunday and Friday are all _____ of the week.

c. Katy, Mat and Ravi are all _____ at my school.

d. July, August and September are all _____ of the year.

e. Glasgow, London and Cardiff are all _____ in Britain.

f. Mars, Jupiter and Venus are all _____ in our solar system.

2. Use the proper nouns in the box to complete the story.

> Rover   July   Tuesday   Michael
> Sea World   Joanna   Devon

"Next _____, which is the 15th of _____, is my birthday," said

_____. "My parents are going to take me to _____ in

_____ as a treat. My sister, _____, is also coming

but I am going to leave my dog, _____, at home."

Collective Nouns

Name _____

Collective nouns are the names we use for collections of things.

1. Choose a collective noun from the box to write on the line under each drawing.

> bunch   flock   herd   forest   swarm

a. a _____ of cattle

b. a _____ of grapes

c. a _____ of bees

d. a _____ of trees

e. a _____ of birds

2. Use the words in the box to complete the story.

> album   string   pack   brood   bundle   box

In the old box Sally found a _____ of pearls, a _____ of matches and an old _____ of playing cards. Suddenly, as she lifted a _____ of rags, she saw an _____ of stamps. She grabbed the stamps and raced outside to show her father who was feeding the _____ of chickens that had just hatched.

3. Write the word from the box that names each group or class of things.

> fruit   birds   furniture   insects

a. hawks, eagles and doves _____

b. ants, bees and grasshoppers _____

c. apples, pears and bananas _____

d. tables, chairs and benches _____

Collective Nouns

Name _____

**Collective nouns are the names we use
for collections of things.**

1. Write each noun under its collective heading.

> banana   desk   apple   stool   table   pear
> chair   zebra   dove   giraffe   lion
> swan   horse   duck   eagle   peach

Animals   Birds   Fruit   Furniture

_____   _____   _____   _____

_____   _____   _____   _____

_____   _____   _____   _____

_____   _____   _____   _____

2. Write the word from the box that names each group or class of things.

> people   countries   meat   vegetables   flowers   fruit

a. uncle, aunt, boy and girl _____

b. daisy, rose, daffodil and pansy _____

c. lettuce, turnip, potato and bean _____

d. chop, sausage, steak and beef _____

e. lemon, orange, lime and apricot _____

f. Australia, China, Vietnam and Spain _____

3. Match each collective noun to the group it names.

> cards   people   grapes   beads   students   footballers

a. a class of _____   d. a pack of_____

b. a team of _____   e. a crowd of_____

c. a bunch of_____   f. a string of_____

Plural Nouns

Name _____

Singular nouns refer to one person, place or thing.
Plural nouns refer to more than one person, place or thing.

1. Write the correct word on the line.

a. Mr Smith has two _____ on his arm. **(watch watches)**

b. Shaheen has three blue _____ . **(dress dresses)**

c. The gardener cut down all the _____ . **(branch branches)**

d. The fairy gave me three _____ . **(wish wishes)**

e. My mother asked me to bring her all the _____ .
(brush   brushes)

f. There are a lot of _____ at our school. **(class classes)**

2. Circle the plural nouns. Hint: there might be more than one in a sentence.

a. The men swept the leaves.

b. The cats climbed the fence.

c. The birds flew into the trees.

d. The horses ate some grass.

e. The donkeys kicked the gate.

f. The buses stopped at all the schools.

3. Write the plural nouns.

a. one child, two _____

b. one ball, four _____

c. one boat, two _____

d. one mouse, four _____

e. one monkey, two _____

f. one man, four _____

Plural Nouns

Name _____

Singular nouns refer to one person, place or thing.
Plural nouns refer to more than one person, place or thing.

1. Write the plural nouns on the lines.

a. one toy, two _____

b. one city, two _____

c. one lady, two _____

d. one puppy, two _____

e. one trolley, two _____

f. one party, two _____

2. Complete each sentence by writing the singular of the noun in brackets.

a. I killed the _____ that landed on the cake. **(flies)**

b. I saw a _____ in the paddock. **(donkeys)**

c. Ian ate the _____ for lunch. **(jellies)**

d. The ice-cream had a _____ on top. **(cherries)**

e. The _____ looks clear today. **(skies)**

f. I saw a laser _____ hit his body. **(rays)**

3. Complete each sentence by writing the plural of the noun in brackets.

a. There were three _____ in the forest. **(wolf)**

b. The waiter put all the _____ on the table. **(knife)**

c. The police caught the three _____ . **(thief)**

d. Put the books on the _____ . **(shelf)**

e. We cut the oranges into _____ . **(half)**

f. It is said that a cat has nine _____ . **(life)**

Nouns – Revision

Name _____

1. Write a collective noun in each space.

a. a _____ of footballers

b. a _____ of matches

c. a _____ of cards

d. a _____ of students

e. a _____ of birds

f. a _____ of bees

2. Rewrite the story, writing the underlined words in the plural.

The <u>lion</u> sat under the <u>tree</u> because it was so hot. The <u>fly</u> buzzed around and the <u>lion</u> flicked <u>it</u> with <u>its tail</u>. On the <u>branch</u> of the <u>tree</u> the <u>monkey</u> <u>was</u> nearly asleep. The <u>lion</u> growled loudly and shook <u>its mane</u>.

_____

_____

_____

_____

_____

_____

3. Write the singular nouns.

a. two jellies, one _____

b. two buses, one _____

c. two ladies, one _____

d. two cities, one _____

e. two leaves, one _____

f. two halves, one _____

Answers to Nouns

Answers to page 6

1a countries

1b days

1c students

1d months

1e cities

1f planets

2 Tuesday July Michael Sea World Devon Joanna Rover

Answers to page 7

1a herd

1b bunch

1c swarm

1d forest

1e flock

2 string box pack bundle album brood

3a birds

3b insects

3c fruit

3d furniture

Answers to page 8

1 Animals: zebra giraffe lion horse

Birds: dove swan duck eagle

Fruit: banana apple pear peach

Furniture: desk stool table chair

2a people

2b flowers

2c vegetables

2d meat

2e fruit

2f countries

3a students

3b footballers

3c grapes

3d cards

3e people

3f beads

Answers to page 9

1a watches

1b dresses

1c branches

1d wishes

1e brushes

1f classes

2a men leaves

2b cats

2c birds trees

2d horses

2e donkeys

2f buses schools

3a children

3b balls

3c boats

3d mice

3e monkeys

3f men

Answers to page 10

1a toys

1b cities

1c ladies

1d puppies

1e trolleys

1f parties

2a fly

2b donkey

2c jelly

2d cherry

2e sky

2f ray

3a wolves

3b knives

3c thieves

3d shelves

3e halves

3f lives

Answers to page 11

1a team

1b box

1c pack

1d class

1e flock

1f swarm

2 lions trees flies lions them their tails branches trees monkeys were lions their manes

3a jelly

3b bus

3c lady

3d city

3e leaf

3f half

Introduction to Verbs

National Literacy Strategy objectives

The work on verbs at lower Key Stage 2 focuses on verb agreement and verb tenses, and finding synonyms for particular verbs:

Y3T1 S3: the function of verbs in sentences through:

noticing that sentences cannot make sense without them;

collecting and classifying examples of verbs from reading and own knowledge, e.g. run, chase, sprint; eat, consume, gobble; said, whispered, shrieked;

experimenting with changing simple verbs in sentences and discussing their impact on meaning;

Y3T1 S4: to use verb tenses with increasing accuracy in speaking and writing, e.g. catch/caught, see/saw, go/went etc. Use past tense consistently for narration;

Y3T2 S10: to understand the differences between verbs in the 1st, 2nd and 3rd person, e.g. I/we do, you/you do, he/she/they do/does.

Introducing verbs

The Word level objectives for Vocabulary extension in Year 3 Term 1 also introduce the word synonym and suggest that pupils 'generate synonyms for high frequency words': the exercise on page 15 is therefore a perfect way in to pupils finding alternative verbs for the overworked 'said'.

Tenses were introduced in Key Stage 1, and pupils should now be able to convert text from present to past to future, according to context. Note that 'will' is used here for every form of the future; 'shall' is used less often now, even for emphatic use.

On subject/verb agreement, you can start by just teaching singular and plural agreement, but should then explain the terminology of 1st, 2nd and 3rd person subjects in singular and plural, and how they affect the form of the verb.

Class activities

Encourage children to mime chosen activities and challenge classmates to come up with the verb, in sentence form, that describes what they are doing.

Worksheet answers

Answers are provided on page 20.

Verbs

Name _____

Action verbs express an action we can see. For example: work, run, sit.

1. Unjumble the letters in brackets and write the action verb in the space.

a. I helped Zach_____the dishes. (**awsh**)

b. Please don't_____ the flowers. (**ipck**)

c. Did you _____ your bicycle to school? (**irde**)

d. The children are going to _____from their friends. (**ihde**)

e. He put the sugar in the tea and then began to _____ it. (**tsir**)

f. Be careful the cat does not_____you. (**atchscr**)

2. Add an action verb and a noun to complete each sentence.

Action Verbs	Nouns
rode	soap
rocked	tree
ate	path
washed	cot

a. The giraffe _____the leaves on the tall _____ .

b. The mother gently _____the baby in the _____ .

c. I_____my dirty clothes with _____ and water.

d. Freya _____the horse along the dusty _____ .

Verbs

Saying verbs express a spoken action. For example:
talk, tell, said.

1. Add a saying verb to complete each sentence.

> tell   whisper   screamed   said   talk   yelled

a. The girls began to _____ when the boys came near.

b. The boy_____ across the playground to his friend.

c. The teacher is going to_____ us a story.

d. Ian_____ that he did not do it.

e. I will_____ to you on the phone tonight.

f. The children_____ when they saw the scary monster mask.

2. Write a sentence using each saying verb.

a. shouted _____

   _____

b. whispered _____

   _____

c. talked _____

   _____

d. muttered _____

   _____

Verb Tenses

Name _____

Verbs can tell us when an action is taking place.
If the action is happening now it is called present tense.
I am playing football.
If the action has already happened it is called past tense.
I played football yesterday.
If the action has not yet happened it is called future tense.
I will play football tomorrow.

1. These sentences are written in the present tense. Rewrite them in the past tense.
    The first one has been done for you.

a. I am a cricketer.
                                    I was a cricketer.
    _____

b. Shaheen and Katy are playing soccer.

    _____

c. Mike wants a pizza.

    _____

d. Mr Smith is a popular teacher.

    _____

e. It is good luck to see a black cat.

    _____

f. I am going to netball practice.

    _____

2. On the line, write whether the underlined verb is in the present, past or future tense.

a. I <u>played</u> football yesterday.   _____

b. We <u>will arrive</u> soon.   _____

c. They <u>are</u> the best players.   _____

d. The teacher <u>is</u> talking.   _____

e. We <u>stayed</u> a long time.   _____

f. I <u>will be</u> in the team next year.   _____

Verb Tenses

Name _____

Verbs can tell us when an action is taking place.
If the action is happening now it is called present tense.
I am playing football.
If the action has already happened it is called past tense.
I played football yesterday.
If the action has not yet happened it is called future tense.
I will play football tomorrow.

1. Complete each sentence by writing the past tense of the verb in brackets.

a. Mat_____ the school bell this morning. (**ring**)

b. I_____ my bicycle to school. (**ride**)

c. We_____ many interesting things in the city. (**see**)

d. Raj_____ all the lollies. (**eat**)

e. I_____ a picture of a snake in my book. (**draw**)

f. It_____ very cold. (**is**)

2. Now rewrite the sentences from question 1 in the future tense.

a. _____

b. _____

c. _____

d. _____

e. _____

f. _____

Verb Tenses

Name _____

Verbs can tell us when an action is taking place.
If the action is happening now it is called present tense.
I am playing football.
If the action has already happened it is called past tense.
I played football yesterday.
If the action has not yet happened it is called future tense.
I will play football tomorrow.

Circle all the verbs in the story. Then rewrite the story in the past tense.

I sit down and eat my breakfast. I bite my tongue and it hurts. I am feeling bored so I go outside and walk along the street. In the distance I see a car. I think it is a Toyota. The car comes towards me at great speed. I jump out of the way just in time. I go back inside. I trip over my skateboard in the hallway and crash into the hall cupboard. I stand up and bang my head on the open cupboard door. It is not a good day. I go back to bed.

_____

_____

_____

_____

_____

_____

_____

_____

_____

Subject and Verb Agreement

Name _____

If the subject of a verb is plural (more than one), the verb should also be plural.
The boys are coming down the road.
The girls like ice-cream.
If the subject of a verb is singular (only one), the verb should also be singular.
The boy is coming down the road.
The girl likes ice-cream.

1. Choose the correct verb from the brackets and write it on the line.

a. I saw the boys_____towards the house. (**run runs**)

b. That girl _____in the park. (**play plays**)

c. Every day the lady _____ across the river. (**swim swims**)

d. The children in that class _____ to read books. (**like likes**)

e. After tea, Grandpa _____ in his chair. (**sit sits**)

f. The girls often _____ stories about monsters. (**write writes**)

2. Circle the correct verb in each set of brackets.

This (**is are**) my dog, Rover. He (**is are**) a German Shepherd. German

Shepherds (**is are**) good watchdogs. They (**is are**) big and strong. Rover

(**is are**) black but many German Shepherds (**is are**) a brown colour.

My favourite pets (**is are**) dogs, and I think a German Shepherd (**is are**)

the best dog of all.

Answers to Verbs

Answers to page 14

1a wash

1b pick

1c ride

1d hide

1e stir

1f scratch

2a ate tree

2b rocked cot

2c washed soap

2d rode path

Answers to page 15

1a whisper

1b yelled

1c tell

1d said

1e talk

1f screamed

Answers to page 16

1b Shaheen and Katy were playing soccer.

1c Mike wanted a pizza.

1d Mr Smith was a popular teacher.

1e It was good luck to see a black cat.

1f I was going to netball practice.

2a past

2b future

2c present

2d present

2e past

2f future

Answers to page 17

1a rang

1b rode

1c saw

1d ate

1e drew

1f was

2a Mat will ring the school bell this morning.

2b I will ride my bicycle to school.

2c We will see many interesting things in the city.

2d Raj will eat all the lollies.

2e I will draw a picture of a snake in my book.

2f It will be very cold.

Answers to page 18

I sat down and ate my breakfast. I bit my tongue and it hurt. I was feeling bored so I went outside and walked along the street. In the distance I saw a car. I thought it was a Toyota. The car came towards me at great speed. I jumped out of the way just in time. I went back inside. I tripped over my skateboard in the hallway and crashed into the hall cupboard. I stood up and banged my head on the open cupboard door. It was not a good day. I went back to bed.

Answers to page 19

1a run

1b plays

1c swims

1d like

1e sits

1f write

2 is is are are is are are is

20

Introduction to Adjectives

National Literacy Strategy objectives

Adjectives are first fully defined as a word class in Year 3 Term 2:

Y3T2 S2: the function of adjectives within sentences, through:

identifying adjectives in shared reading;

discussing and defining what they have in common i.e. words which qualify nouns;

experimenting with deleting and substituting adjectives and noting effects on meaning;

collecting and classifying adjectives, e.g. for colours, sizes, moods;

experimenting with the impact of different adjectives through shared writing.

Introducing adjectives

The above sequence provides a logical way of introducing the function of adjectives: locating in shared reading, defining what they do, using and substituting, collecting and experimenting in pupils' own writing.

The spelling of comparative forms of adjectives will also need to be taught, following the rules for any suffix after a particular ending of the root word:

Y3T2 W8: how words change when 'er' and 'est' are added.

Class activities

Place an object in a bag and let children feel the object. Ask them to describe the object to you – It is soft, it is round, it is rubbery and so on.

Write a story, preferably a short joke, on the board. Underline all the nouns. Then ask children to rewrite the story adding adjectives to the nouns.

Look at comparing adjectives by asking a child to come to the front of the room. Then ask a shorter and a taller child up to the front too. Then ask questions such as: Who is the tallest? Who is the shortest? Is Mary taller than Peter? Is Tom smaller than Mary? etc.

Worksheet answers

Answers are provided on page 28.

Adjectives

Name _____

Describing adjectives are used to describe a noun or pronoun.

1. Draw a line to match each describing adjective with a noun.

Describing Adjectives	Nouns
fast	door
open	peach
hard	water
hot	rock
deep	runner
interesting	hair
dark	fire
ripe	book

2. In each sentence, rearrange the jumbled letters to make a describing adjective.

a. Raj is very _____ for his age. (**llta**)

b. This is a very _____ building. (**lod**)

c. Here is a _____ jumper. (**eancl**)

d. This is a piece of _____ wool. (**lbue**)

e. Mat does _____ writing in his book. (**enat**)

f. This is a very _____ river. (**edep**)

Adjectives

**Describing adjectives are used to describe
a noun or pronoun.**

1. Complete each sentence by adding the correct describing adjective from the box.

> tiny   huge   sharp   long   savage   hard

a. I cut the bread with a _____ knife.

b. A mouse is a _____ animal.

c. A giraffe has a _____ neck.

d. A whale is a _____ animal.

e. A tiger is a _____ animal.

f. An old crab has a _____ shell.

2. Add a describing adjective of your own in each space.

Last week a _____ boy and his _____

friend were walking along a _____ street. They looked at

the top of a _____ tree and saw a _____

bird sitting on a _____ branch. The bird swooped down

and landed on a _____ fence where it had started to build

a _____ nest.

Adjectives

Name _____

Describing adjectives are used to describe a noun or pronoun.

1. Write a suitable describing adjective in each space.

a. A _____ girl lifted a _____ table.

b. A _____ dog chased a _____ boy.

c. The _____ cat followed the _____ mouse.

d. It was a _____ day when we went to the _____ forest.

e. A _____ bird laid three _____ eggs in the nest.

f. I put the _____ lock back in the _____ container.

2. Now write two descriptive adjectives to complete these sentences.

a. A teacher should be _____ and _____ .

b. The grass was _____ and _____ .

c. The flowers were _____ and _____ .

d. My dog is _____ and _____ .

e. My best friend is _____ and _____ .

f. A book should be _____ and _____ .

Adjectives

Name _____

**Describing adjectives are used to describe
a noun or pronoun.**

1. Read the passage and circle all the describing adjectives. Then answer the questions below.

My best friend, Chan, has black hair and large, brown eyes. One day he was walking along a busy street bouncing his rubber basketball when he heard a strange noise coming from the top of a tall oak tree. He looked up and on the highest branch he saw a magpie with a broken wing being attacked by a hawk. The hawk was brown and had a strong beak.

a. What are Chan's eyes like? _____

b. How good a friend is Chan to the writer? _____

c. What colour hair does Chan have? _____

d. What type of street was Chan walking along? _____

e. What type of noise did Chan hear? _____

f. What was wrong with the magpie's wing? _____

2. Add an adjective of your own to describe each noun.

a. a _____ teacher

b. a _____ meal

c. a _____ tree

d. a _____ fish

e. a _____ flower

f. a _____ game

Adjectives

_____

Adjectives can change their form to show degrees of comparison.

Positive Degree	Comparative Degree	Superlative Degree
sweet	sweeter	sweetest
muddy	muddier	muddiest
beautiful	more beautiful	most beautiful

1. Write the comparative degree of each adjective in brackets.

a. Mike is_____ than Rahim. (**strong**)

b. Today is_____than yesterday. (**hot**)

c. This apple is_____ than the one you have. (**red**)

d. This table is_____ than that one. (**heavy**)

e. I think I am _____ than you. (**lucky**)

f. This pie is_____ than that one. (**delicious**)

2. Write the superlative degree of each adjective in brackets.

a. This is the_____ day all year. (**hot**)

b. This is the _____ place to hide. (**safe**)

c. Tom is the_____ boy in the school. (**reliable**)

d. A Clydesdale is the _____horse of all. (**big**)

e. Joe is the_____ person in the class. (**noisy**)

f. Ms Smith is the _____ person I know. (**brave**)

Adjectives

Name _____

Adjectives can change their form to show degrees of comparison.

Positive Degree	Comparative Degree	Superlative Degree
sweet	sweeter	sweetest
muddy	muddier	muddiest
beautiful	more beautiful	most beautiful

1. Complete the table.

Positive Degree	Comparative Degree	Superlative Degree
smooth		
		thinnest
	luckier	
wise		
	more delicate	
		greenest
good	better	

2. Complete each sentence by choosing the correct adjective degree from the brackets.

a. Tom is _____ than Shaheen. (**older oldest**)

b. A cat is a _____ pet than a dog. (**better best**)

c. This summer is the _____ one I have ever known. (**hotter hottest**)

d. Today is _____ than it was yesterday. (**colder coldest**)

Answers to Adjectives

Answers to page 22

1 fast runner

open door

hard rock

hot fire

deep water

interesting book

dark hair

ripe peach

2a tall

2b old

2c clean

2d blue

2e neat

2f deep

Answers to page 23

1a sharp

1b tiny

1c long

1d huge

1e savage

1f hard

Answers to page 25

1 best black large brown one busy rubber strange tall highest broken brown strong

a large and brown

b best

c black

d busy

e strange

f it was broken

Answers to page 26

1a stronger

1b hotter

1c redder

1d heavier

1e luckier

1f more delicious

2a hottest

2b safest

2c most reliable

2d biggest

2e noisiest

2f bravest

Answers to page 27

1 smoother smoothest

thin thinner

lucky luckiest

wiser wisest

delicate most delicate

green greener

best

2a older

2b better

2c hottest

2d colder

Introduction to Adverbs

National Literacy Strategy objectives

Adverbs are introduced in Year 4 Term 1:

Y4T1 S4: to identify adverbs and understand their functions in sentences through:

identifying common adverbs with 'ly' suffix and discussing their impact on the meaning of sentences; noticing where they occur in sentences and how they are used to qualify the meaning of verbs;

collecting and classifying examples of adverbs, e.g. for speed: swiftly, rapidly, sluggishly; light: brilliantly, dimly;

investigating the effects of substituting adverbs in clauses or sentences, e.g. They left the house _____ ly;

using adverbs with greater discrimination in own writing.

Introducing adverbs

Whereas adjectives say more about a noun, adverbs usually add to a verb.

Often adverbs end with the suffix 'ly', and are placed close to the verb.

When adding the suffix, you follow the same spelling rules as when adding any other suffix to that root word.

There are three main kinds of adverbs: those of place (where), time (when) and manner (how).

As with adjectives, adverbs can be extended into a comparative form (more) or superlative form (most).

Class activities

Ask children to provide one word to replace a group of words in a sentence that is written on the board.
Mike always drives <u>in a fast way</u>.
Mike always drives <u>quickly</u>.

Write adverbs on cards and hand them around the class so that each child has one. Then read out the beginning of a sentence, and ask the children to hold up their card if they think it is appropriate to complete it.

Worksheet answers

Answers are provided on page 36.

Adverbs

Some adverbs look like adjectives. You can tell they are adverbs if they add meaning to verbs, adjectives and other adverbs. If they add meaning to a noun, they are adjectives.

1. Circle the adverb to complete each sentence.

a. The girls played (**happy happily**) in the gymnasium.

b. The teacher laughed (**loud loudly**) at my joke.

c. Ravi ran (**quick quickly**).

d. I jumped the fence (**easy easily**).

e. The teacher corrected our work (**careful carefully**).

f. Jo held her trophy (**proud proudly**).

2. Change the word in brackets into an adverb to complete each sentence.

a. Ben can swim _____ . (**strong**)

b. Ali cried _____ . (**sad**)

c. The lady sang _____ . (**loud**)

d. The mother sang_____ to her child. (**soft**)

e. The teacher asked us to work _____ . (**neat**)

f. The train came _____ into the station. (**slow**)

Adverbs

Name _____

An adverb is a word that adds meaning to a verb, an adjective or another adverb. Adverbs of place show where something happened:
I told him to come *here*.

1. Use a place adverb from the box to complete each sentence.

(out   here   there   somewhere   everywhere   near)

a. The supermarket is not far, in fact it is quite _____ .

b. The teacher said to put the book _____ .

c. The accident occurred right _____ .

d. Ian came in as we went _____ .

e. When the jar dropped, the lollies scattered _____ .

f. I was sure I put my guitar _____ .

2. Write sentences of your own that use these words as adverbs of place.

a. above
_____

b. downstairs
_____

c. in
_____

d. outside
_____

e. nowhere
_____

f. behind
_____

Adverbs

Name _____

An adverb is a word that adds meaning to a verb, an adjective or another adverb. Adverbs of time show when something happened:
He played *yesterday*.

1. Choose a time adverb from the box to replace the underlined words in each sentence.

> later   now   yesterday   often   today   soon

a. Mike should arrive <u>in a short time</u>. _____

b. Don't wait for a moment, do it <u>straight away</u>. _____

c. We went swimming <u>the day before today</u>. _____

d. We are going camping <u>the day it is now</u>. _____

e. There's no panic. You can finish it <u>in the future</u>. _____

f. Shaheen skips <u>lots of times</u>. _____

2. Write sentences of your own that use these words as adverbs of time.

a. seldom

_____

b. never

_____

c. then

_____

d. already

_____

e. before

_____

f. late

_____

Adverbs

An adverb is a word that adds meaning to a verb, an adjective or another adverb. Adverbs of manner show how something happened: He worked *quietly*.

1. Choose an adverb of manner from the box to complete each sentence.

noisily   easily   slowly   greedily   silently   gently

a. The starving dog ate the meat _____ .

b. Mother put our baby to bed _____ .

c. The cat crept _____ after the mouse.

d. The fastest runner _____won the race.

e. The boy with the broken leg walked _____ down the street.

f. When the teacher left, the class worked _____ .

2. Write sentences of your own that use these words as adverbs of manner.

a. softly

_____

b. quickly

_____

c. carefully

_____

d. sadly

_____

e. badly

_____

f. happily

_____

Adverbs

Name _____

An adverb is a word that adds meaning to a verb, an adjective or another adverb.
- **Adverbs of manner show *how* something happened.**
- **Adverbs of place show *where* something happened.**
- **Adverbs of time show *when* something happened.**

1. Look at the underlined adverb and write whether it tells how, where or when.

a. I found it <u>there</u>. _____

b. We crossed the busy road <u>carefully</u>. _____

c. I asked her to come <u>here</u>. _____

d. We should cut the lawn <u>today</u>. _____

e. Are you playing football <u>tomorrow</u>? _____

f. The child sulked <u>sadly</u>. _____

2. Choose the correct adverb to complete each sentence.

> here   now   there   soon   loudly   quickly

a. The plants are growing _____ . **(how)**

b. I will see you _____ . **(when)**

c. Please come over _____ . **(where)**

d. The angry dog barked _____ . **(how)**

e. Put it down _____ . **(where)**

f. I want you to do it right _____ . **(when)**

Adverbs

Name _____

Adverbs can change their form to show degrees of comparison.

Positive Degree	Comparative Degree	Superlative Degree
hard	harder	hardest
softly	more softly	softest
well	better	best

1. Fill the spaces with the correct adverb from the brackets.

a. Raj jumps_____ than Tony. (**higher highest**)

b. This apple tastes_____ than that one. (**better best**)

c. The red car starts_____ than yours. (**more easily most easily**)

d. Take this pencil. It writes the _____ of all. (**better best**)

e. Out of all the children it was Meg who ran _____ .
    (**faster fastest**)

f. A dog eats_____ than a cat. (**more most**)

g. Asha played_____ than Peter. (**longer longest**)

h. Of all the children Tom sang the _____ . (**louder loudest**)

2. Put the words in brackets in their correct order in the sentences.

a. Mike did his work well. Sam did his work_____ . Zach did
    his work_____ of all. (**best better**)

b. This red car travels _____ . Does the blue car go
    _____ ? Of the red, blue and green car, which travels the
    _____ ? (**faster fast fastest**)

Answers to Adverbs

Answers to page 30

1a happily

1b loudly

1c quickly

1d easily

1e carefully

1f proudly

2a strongly

2b sadly

2c loudly

2d softly

2e neatly

2f slowly

Answers to page 31

1a near

1b there

1c here

1d out

1e everywhere

1f somewhere

Answers to page 32

1a soon

1b now

1c yesterday

1d today

1e later

1f often

Answers to page 33

1a greedily

1b gently

1c silently

1d easily

1e slowly

1f noisily

Answers to page 34

1a Where

1b How

1c Where

1d When

1e When

1f How

2a quickly

2b soon

2c here

2d loudly

2e there

2f now

Answers to page 35

1a higher

1b better

1c more easily

1d best

1e fastest

1f more

1g longer

1h loudest

2a better best

2b fast faster fastest

Introduction to Prepositions

National Literacy Strategy objectives

Prepositions are not introduced in the National Literacy Strategy until Year 5, but teachers may want to introduce them earlier, especially as prepositions relating to space and measurement are introduced in Numeracy by this stage.

Introducing prepositions

The starting-point for prepositions is usually descriptions in relation to space: above, below, beside etc.

You can then progress to prepositions that describe other relationships to nouns, e.g. prepositions of *by, with* or *from*.

Class activities

Ask questions about a picture – Where is the rabbit? Where is the car? Encourage children to answer using a preposition to say where things are.

Ask two children to come out to the front and get one to give the other a set of instructions to follow. Stand <u>by</u> the door, put the book <u>on</u> the table.

Play preposition opposites: You say: The snake crawled <u>over</u> the rock. And children might say: The snake crawled <u>under</u> the rock.

Worksheet answers

Answers are provided on page 42.

Prepositions

Name _____

Prepositions show the relationship of a noun or a pronoun to another word in the sentence. They are usually followed by a noun or a pronoun.

1. Use a preposition from the box to complete each sentence.

> through   during   in   over   up   under

a. There were six eggs _____ the magpie's nest.

b. A lot of homes were damaged _____ the storm.

c. The kangaroo jumped _____ the fence.

d. The children walked _____ the forest.

e. The little kitten was _____ the table.

f. She was the first person to climb all the way _____ the mountain.

2. Circle the correct preposition in brackets.

a. Did they moan (**for   at**) you for breaking the window?

b. The teacher was angry (**with   at**) me.

c. The pear fell (**off   from**) the tree.

d. The bottle is full (**of   with**) water.

e. Let's sit here and wait (**after   for**) Ian.

f. Karen fell (**off   into**) the pool.

Prepositions

Name _____

Prepositions show the relationship of a noun or a pronoun to another word in the sentence. They are usually followed by a noun or a pronoun.

1. Use the opposite preposition to fill each space.

| over | above | after | around | off | outside |

a. The dog crawled <u>under</u> the bush.

The dog jumped _____ the bush.

b. We went <u>inside</u> the classroom.

We went _____ the classroom.

c. We left <u>before</u> the bell rang.

We left_____the bell rang.

d. I looked at the hole <u>below</u> me.

I looked at the stars_____ me.

e. The children sat <u>on</u> the branch.

The children fell _____ the branch.

f. We rowed <u>across</u> the lake.

We rowed _____ the lake.

2. Use a different preposition to complete each sentence.

a. Walk_____the door.

b. Jump _____the seat.

c. Look _____the book.

d. Sit_____your sister.

e. Run_____the lawn.

f. Come_____me.

Prepositions

Name _____

Prepositions show the relationship of a noun or a pronoun to another word in the sentence. They are usually followed by a noun or a pronoun.

1. Add a preposition of your own to complete each sentence.

a. Mat ran all the way _____ the shop.

b. The dog sleeps _____ a kennel.

c. The frightened kitten hid _____ the table.

d. I saw him running _____ the street.

e. She leant the shovel _____ the wall.

f. The cat climbed quickly _____ the tree.

2. Make sentences by combining the groups of words in the boxes.
   If you need more space, use the back of the sheet.

The horses are	above	the kennel.
The boys are playing	in	the house.
The dog is sleeping	under	the park.
The bird is flying	on	the garden.
The girls are picnicking	beside	the stables.
	near	

_____

_____

_____

_____

_____

40

Prepositions

Prepositions show the relationship of a noun or a pronoun to another word in the sentence. They are usually followed by a noun or a pronoun.

1. Use a different preposition to complete each sentence.

a. A bird is sitting _____ the nest.

b. A rabbit is hopping _____ the fence.

c. The snake is sliding _____ its hole.

d. A cat is sleeping _____ the table.

e. Ellen goes_____ her grandma's every weekend.

f. The roots of a tree are _____ the branches.

2. Read the story. Circle the prepositions.

The children swam across the lake and then walked between
the pine trees into the forest. After they had walked through
the forest they walked down the path that led to the beach.
When they reached the beach they ran towards the water.
They dived off the rocks into the rock pool.

Answers to Prepositions

Answers to page 38

1a in

1b during

1c over

1d through

1e under

1f up

2a at

2b with

2c off

2d of

2e for

2f into

Answers to page 39

1a over

1b outside

1c after

1d above

1e off

1f around

Answers to page 41

2 across between into through down to towards off into

Introduction to Pronouns

Since the National Literacy Strategy introduces the terminology for 1st, 2nd and 3rd person with both verbs and pronouns, the pronouns can best be taught through the following grid:

	Subject Singular	Subject Plural	Object Singular	Object Plural	Possessive Singular	Possessive Plural
1st Person	I	we	me	us	mine	ours
2nd Person	you	you	you	you	yours	yours
3rd Person	he, she, it	they	him, her, it	them	his, hers, its	theirs

You could draw up a blank grid with these headings, and ask pupils to fill the boxes.

Pupils can practise the difference between subject and object on page 47.

(Note that 'who' and 'that' are also pronouns, whereas 'my', 'your', 'her' are strictly possessive adjectives rather than pronouns.)

Class activities

Use a simple nursery rhyme such as Little Miss Muffet. Recite: Little Miss Muffet sat on Miss Muffet's tuffet, eating Miss Muffet's curds and whey. Ask children to suggest a pronoun to replace all the Miss Muffet's.

Write out a short passage, in large letters on a big sheet of paper, with all the pronouns missing. Write all the missing pronouns on pieces of card and ask the children to work in teams to work out where they should go.

Worksheet answers

Answers are provided on page 50.

Pronouns

Name _____

Pronouns are words that take the place of nouns. Choose a pronoun from the box to fill in these blanks.

me	you	it	him	her	us	them
he	she	we	they	their	its	your
my	that	who	I	our		

a. Sharm left _____ in the classroom.

b. Ian said _____ could run faster.

c. The cat was licking _____ fur.

d. There is the dog _____ bit the postal worker.

e. We did not know _____ had stolen the money.

f. Katy told me that _____ was leaving right away.

Pronouns

Pronouns are words that take the place of nouns.

Rewrite the story using pronouns to replace the underlined nouns.

One day Sharm and Sharm's father went to the zoo. Sharm and Sharm's father travelled to the zoo in a bus. Sharm's father took Sharm to the zoo because it was Sharm's birthday and Sharm had always wanted to see the tigers that Sharm had read about in the newspaper. The tigers were brought to Britain in the hope that the tigers would breed.

_____

_____

_____

_____

_____

_____

_____

_____

Pronouns

Pronouns are words that take the place of nouns.

1. Circle the correct pronoun.

a. The birds flew away when I scared (**those them**).

b. That belongs to Raj, please give it back to (**him he**).

c. Are you going to come with (**I me**)?

d. Did (**us you**) get the milk?

e. Mary can't come because (**her she**) is ill.

f. Do you think (**them they**) will help us?

2. Replace the underlined words with a pronoun. Rewrite the sentence.

a. The teacher said <u>the teacher</u> had a sore throat.

_____

b. The boy told his friend to get <u>the boy</u> an ice-cream.

_____

c. Neema's mother asked <u>Neema</u> to clean up the bathroom.

_____

d. Michael and I stopped when <u>Michael and I</u> became tired.

_____

Pronouns

Name _____

**Sometimes it is difficult to decide when to use *I*
or *me* in a sentence. If in doubt, divide the sentence
into two short sentences.**
• *Mike is going to the circus. I am going to the circus.*
So the correct usage is: *Mike and I are going to the circus.*
**• *Ling told Sally to get off the grass. Ling told me to
get off the grass.***
**So the correct usage is: *Ling told Sally and me to get
off the grass.***

Circle the correct pronoun.

a. Ravi and (**I me**) are going to the party.

b. Aunty Tanya sent presents to Katy and (**I me**).

c. Between you and (**I me**), I think the teacher is wrong.

d. There was trouble coming for Kyle and (**I me**).

e. I was sure that Tom and (**I me**) were in trouble.

f. Asha and (**I me**) received letters from Uncle Raj.

g. Zach and (**I me**) are going to the movies.

h. Susan asked Shane and (**I me**) to visit.

i. Mum, Dad and (**I me**) are going shopping for a new car.

j. Would you like to come to the pool with Mat and (**I me**)?

Pronouns

Name _____

Pronouns are words that take the place of nouns.

1. List all the pronouns.

One day, when I was out walking with some friends, I saw Lily and Neema crossing the road. They said they were going to the park. We said we would go with them so Lily ran home to get a football. She said we had to be careful with it because it was a present from Uncle Harry who is a famous footballer.

_____

_____

_____

_____

_____

2. Colour red those boxes that contain a pronoun.

dog	me	silly	it	him	running
I	happy	he	ten	paper	them
pencil	us	down	they	her	your
we	old	she	penguin	it	sink
book	you	blue	them	cup	their

Pronouns

Name _____

Pronouns are words that take the place of nouns.

1. Add a pronoun in each space.

a. These books belong to me. These books are _____.

b. Does the piano belong to her? Is the piano _____?

c. These cups belong to us. These cups are _____.

d. The horse belongs to them. The horse is _____.

e. You must take responsibility. The responsibility is _____.

2. Circle the correct pronoun.

a. This is the house (**that whose**) Jack built.

b. I saw the boy (**who which**) saved the drowning lady.

c. Do you know (**whose who**) car that is?

d. Is this the hen (**which who**) lays the large eggs?

e. Do you know the girl (**who whose**) won the gold medal?

f. Did you help the man (**who whose**) leg was broken in the accident?

Answers to Pronouns

Answers to page 45

her They He her her
she she they

Answers to page 46

1a them

1b him

1c me

1d you

1e she

1f they

2a he/she

2b him

2c her

2d we

Answers to page 47

a I

b me

c me

d me

e I

f I

g I

h me

i I

j me

Answers to page 48

1 I I I They they We
we them She we it it

2

me it him

I he them

us they her your

we she it

you them their

Answers to page 49

1a mine

1b hers

1c ours

1d theirs

1e yours

2a that

2b who

2c whose

2d which

2e who

2f whose

Introduction to Connectives

National Literacy Strategy objectives

Although connectives are a grammatical word class in their own right, by Key Stage 2 they are logically treated as a function under Sentence construction:

Y3T3 S5: how sentences can be joined in more complex ways through using a widening range of conjunctions in addition to *and* and *then*, e.g. if, so, while, though, since, when;

Y3T3 S6: to investigate through reading and writing how words and phrases can signal time sequences, e.g. first, then, after, meanwhile, from, where.

Introducing connectives

As pupils' non-fiction writing composition develops, they will need more sophisticated ways of linking arguments in their sentences; e.g. in recounts and persuasive writing, the linking of ideas is vital to the structure of their message.

It is also worth studying how connectives affect the word order and the punctuation of a sentence, e.g. in the answers to page 55.

Class activities

Provide children with exercises in which they use a given connective to join pairs of sentences. For example, use 'but' to join sentences.
Mike is tall. Tom is short.
A fire is hot. Ice is cold.

Carry out a connective search with a passage of text, such as a familiar story or a poem that you have already read. Ask children to read the text and circle any connectives they spot.

Worksheet answers

Answers are provided on page 56.

Connectives

Name _____

Connectives are joining words. They are used to join words and groups of words.

1. Use the words in the box to complete the sentences.

when	before	and	because

a. Mike did not come _____ he was feeling ill.

b. Sharm boiled the eggs _____ Ling cut the bread.

c. We must leave here _____ it begins to rain.

d. The birds flew away _____ they heard the sound of the guns.

2. Join each pair of sentences using the word in the brackets.

a. John could not lift the box. It was too heavy. (**because**)

_____

b. We will have water shortages. It is a hot summer. (**if**)

_____

c. I have not heard from him. I told him to go home. (**since**)

_____

d. We won the match. Our best players were unable to play. (**although**)

_____

Connectives

Name _____

Connectives are joining words. They are used to join words and groups of words.

1. Choose a word from the box to complete each sentence.

> because   when   until   unless   and   if

a. We must wait here_____ our parents arrive.

b. The baby began to cry_____ the little boy pinched him.

c. The thief stole the money _____ he wanted to buy a motor-bike.

d. The fish will not bite_____ you keep making all that noise.

e. I dug up the soil _____ Sally raked it over.

f. You will not get in the team_____ you practise much harder.

2. Make up as many sentences as you can by combining the groups of words in the boxes. If you need more space, write your sentences on the back of the sheet.

Sally giggled	because	her parents said it
Sally cried	although	she would be alright.
Sally didn't come	when	he missed the bus.
Chan laughed	until	she was not feeling well.
Tom yelled		the bus broke down.

_____

_____

_____

_____

Connectives

Name _____

Connectives are joining words. They are used to join words and groups of words.

1. Add a connective to complete each sentence.

a. I missed the bus _____ I got up late.

b. The sun is shining _____ it is starting to snow.

c. Ali cleaned her teeth _____ went to bed.

d. _____ he broke his toy, the little boy began to cry.

e. We had a swim _____ we went to the beach.

f. _____ you do not hurry, you will be late.

2. Add a conjunction in each space.

Last week Raj _____ John did not go to the match

_____ they were not feeling well. They had not been

feeling well _____ they ate some hamburgers they had

bought down the street. Their parents told them they had to stay

at home _____ they were better. The boys agreed with

their parents _____ they both wished they could have

seen the match.

Connectives

Name _____

Connectives are joining words. They are used to join words and groups of words.

On the first line, join the sentences by using a connective in the middle. On the second line, join the sentences by using a connective at the beginning.

a. We had a bath. We arrived home.

_____

_____

b. We ate a sandwich. It was lunchtime.

_____

_____

c. She did not come. She was grounded by her parents.

_____

_____

d. We still felt cold. We lit a fire.

_____

_____

e. Ling washed her hands. She ate her lunch.

_____

_____

f. The train was late. We still arrived on time.

_____

_____

Answers to Connectives

Answers to page 52

1a because

1b and

1c before

1d when

Answers to page 53

1a until

1b when

1c because

1d if

1e and

1f unless

Answers to page 54

1a because

1b although

1c then

1d Because

1e when

1f If

2 and because since until although

Answers to page 55

a We had a bath after we arrived home.

Before we had a bath, we arrived home.

b We ate a sandwich when it was lunchtime.

When we ate a sandwich it was lunchtime.

c She did not come because she was grounded by her parents.

Because she was grounded by her parents, she did not come.

d We still felt cold so we lit a fire.

Because we still felt cold, we lit a fire.

e Ling washed her hands before she ate her lunch.

After Ling washed her hands, she ate her lunch.

f The train was late, yet we still arrived on time.

Although the train was late, we still arrived on time.

Introduction to Sentences

National Literacy Strategy objectives

The references to sentence construction are all about building units of sense, through understanding the use of punctuation, of connectives, and word order.

Introducing sentences

The exercises given start by stressing the need for a verb, or complete part of a verb, to make a sentence complete. This is probably a good rule to teach, so that pupils will understand how they can bend that rule later.

They then introduce the terminology of subject and predicate, and although this is not required by the National Literacy Strategy, again it is a useful aid to understanding sentence construction.

Finally, the pages on clauses act as a bridge to the subsequent section on different kinds of clauses.

Class activities

Write a jumbled sentence on the board.
lives dog a kennel in a
Challenge children to unjumble it. Use very short sentences to start with and use longer ones as children become more confident.

Ask children to match up the beginnings of sentences with the best endings.

Search through newspapers and cut out headline words. Then ask children to create their own sentences using the words, and paste them onto paper.

Write a sentence on the board and then ask children to rearrange the words to make the sentence mean the opposite.
The bull chased the boy.   *The boy chased the bull.*

Worksheet answers

Answers are provided on page 64.

Sentences

Name _____

A sentence must make sense and must contain a verb.

1. Circle the verb in each of these sentences.

a. I like dogs and cats.

b. Will you leave now?

c. Take that puppy out of here.

d. Mike has five hats in his wardrobe.

e. Tom's mother bought a new car.

f. Ling had her birthday party on Friday.

2. Complete each sentence by adding a suitable verb.

a. The dog _____ a rabbit.

b. Rebecca and Asha _____ the same coloured dress

to the party.

c. The rabbit _____ under the fence.

d. James _____ his new shoes to school.

e. Did you _____ the washing this morning?

f. My friend _____ in Wattle Street.

Sentences

Name _____

A sentence must make sense and must contain a verb.

Add a word to complete each sentence. Write the sentence on the line.

a. Last night it heavily.

_____

b. Have you ever to the lake?

_____

c. At the seaside we every day.

_____

d. Why did you that small log?

_____

e. My dog can loudly.

_____

f. Ravi has already this book.

_____

g. My best friend a motor-bike.

_____

h. I the flowers in a vase.

_____

i. The truck down the street.

_____

j. We all the way to the park.

_____

Sentences

Name _____

**A sentence has a part that tells who or what did something
(subject) and a part that tells what they did (predicate).**

1. Draw lines to match each subject to its correct predicate.

A pencil   makes us thirsty.

A car   is a beautiful flower.

Hot weather   is used to write with.

A dentist   has roots and branches.

A lion   looks at our teeth.

A tree   has four wheels.

A giant   is a type of large cat.

A rose   is very large.

2. Add a subject to each predicate.

a. _____ fell into the water.

b. _____ have a new car.

c. _____ feed my puppy every day.

d. _____ won the match at the weekend.

Sentences

Name _____

A sentence has a part that tells who or what did something (subject) and a part that tells what they did (predicate).

1. These sentences have been muddled. Rewrite each one with the correct subject and predicate.

Our teacher crowed loudly at six o'clock.
The kitten was riding his new bicycle.
A key is yellow when it is ripe.
A banana is used to open and lock doors.
The cockerel read us a book about dinosaurs.
Mike was spinning around and trying to catch his tail.

a. _____

b. _____

c. _____

d. _____

e. _____

f. _____

2. Add a predicate to each subject.

a. The lion _____.

b. The police officer _____.

c. The teacher _____.

d. The apple _____.

Sentences

Name _____

A simple sentence is made up of one clause. It contains a verb and makes sense on its own.
I washed the dishes.
A compound sentence is made up of two or more main clauses joined by a connective.
I washed the dishes and Bill dried them.
A complex sentence is made up of a main clause and a subordinate or dependent clause.
I saw the lady who broke the eggs.

After each sentence write whether it is simple, compound or complex.

a. The old man hobbled down the street.

_____

b. I ate an orange and I ate an apple.

_____

c. We will go inside if it begins to rain.

_____

d. The police officer caught the thief who stole the jewels.

_____

e. I have read ten books this year.

_____

f. The hamburgers are delicious and the pizza is too.

_____

g. We went to the zoo and saw the lions.

_____

h. I want to see that film.

_____

Sentences

Name _____

A simple sentence is made up of one clause. It contains a verb and makes sense on its own.
I washed the dishes.
A compound sentence is made up of two or more main clauses joined by a connective.
I washed the dishes and Bill dried them.
A complex sentence is made up of a main clause and a subordinate or dependent clause.
I saw the lady who broke the eggs.

1. Complete these simple sentences by adding words of your own.

a. The large dog _____ .

b. The bus driver _____ .

2. Complete these compound sentences by adding words of your own.

a. The girls were _____ and the boys were

_____ .

b. I found a _____ and I found some _____ .

3. Complete these complex sentences by adding words of your own.

a. The picnic was lots of fun _____ the rain began.

b. The house _____ is near the station is very old.

4. Make up a simple, compound and complex sentence of your own.

a. Simple: _____

b. Compound: _____

c. Complex: _____

Answers to Sentences

Answers to page 58

1a like

1b leave

1c Take

1d has

1e bought

1f had

Suggested answers:

2a chased

2b wore

2c jumped

2d brought

2e do

2f lives

Suggested answers to page 59

a Last night it rained heavily.

b Have you ever been to the lake?

c At the seaside we swim every day.

d Why did you chop that small log?

e My dog can bark loudly.

f Ravi has already read this book.

g My best friend has a motor-bike.

h I put the flowers in a vase.

i The truck drove down the street.

j We all know the way to the park.

Answers to page 60

1 A pencil is used to write with.

A car has four wheels.

Hot weather makes us thirsty.

A dentist looks at our teeth.

A lion is a type of large cat.

A tree has roots and branches.

A giant is very large.

A rose is a beautiful flower.

Answers to page 61

1a Our teacher read us a book about dinosaurs.

1b The kitten was spinning around and trying to catch his tail.

1c A key is used to open and lock doors.

1d A banana is yellow when it is ripe.

1e The cockerel crowed loudly at six o'clock.

1f Mike was riding his new bicycle.

Answers to page 62

a simple

b compound

c compound

d complex

e simple

f compound

g compound

h simple

Phrases: Introduction and Answers

Phrases are simply groups of words without a verb. This section gives examples of phrases used as adjectives and adverbs. The final page explains how they can perform the function of an adverb, or an adjective, or a noun, which will help pupils' general grammatical awareness.

Answers to page 66

1a blind

1b bald

1c now

1d quickly

1e carefully

1f hilly

2 inside the house/ outside the house

in the front/at the back

in the morning/ after lunch

down the steps/ up the stairs

during the day/at night

in a polite way/in a rude manner

Answers to page 67

1a in the cage

1b with long black hair

1c before dinner

1d across the sky

1e at the supermarket

1f into the pool

2a into its burrow

2b searching for food

2c just before sunrise

2d along the road

2e under the tree

2f with sunglasses

Answers to page 68

1a when

1b where

1c how

1d where

1e when

1f where

Answers to page 69

1a very quickly

1b at the school camp

1c with both hands

1d during the afternoon

1e in the cage

1f after the film

Answers to page 70

a adverb

b adjective

c noun

d noun

e adjective

f adverb

g adverb

h noun

i adjective

Phrases

Name _____

A phrase is a group of words that has no finite verb (a verb with its subject).

1. After each phrase write a word from the box that has a similar meaning.

> carefully   quickly   blind   hilly   bald   now

a. without sight _____

b. without hair _____

c. at this moment _____

d. at a great rate _____

e. with great care _____

f. with plenty of hills _____

2. Draw lines to link the phrases that have opposite meanings.

inside the house	in a rude manner
in the front	after lunch
in the morning	up the stairs
down the steps	at night
during the day	at the back
in a polite way	outside the house

Phrases

A phrase is a group of words that has no finite verb (a verb with its subject).

1. Choose the best phrase from the box to complete each sentence.

at the supermarket	before dinner	in the cage
into the pool	across the sky	with long black hair

a. Ling put the bird back _____ .

b. The young girl _____ is my cousin.

c. I washed my hands _____ .

d. The large jet roared _____ .

e. We bought some milk _____ .

f. Max dived from the board _____ .

2. Underline the phrases in these sentences.

a. The rabbit dived into its burrow.

b. The monkey climbed the tree searching for food.

c. We left camp just before sunrise.

d. The car sped along the road.

e. There are lots of mushrooms under the tree.

f. The man with sunglasses is a film star.

Phrases

A phrase is a group of words that has no finite verb (a verb with its subject). Some phrases do the work of an adverb. They tell *how, when* or *where* an action happens.

1. Look at each underlined phrase. Write *how* if it tells how an action happens, *when* if it tells when an action happens, or *where* if it tells where an action happens.

a. We will leave <u>before it is dark</u>.   _____

b. We walked <u>through the long grass</u>.   _____

c. The teacher spoke to us <u>with great care</u>.   _____

d. I can jump <u>over that fence</u>.   _____

e. I play netball <u>during the week</u>.   _____

f. Asha put the box <u>on the table</u>.   _____

2. Write a sentence of your own using each adverbial phrase.

a. just before sunset

_____

b. near the school

_____

c. on his front lawn

_____

d. until ten o'clock

_____

Phrases

Name _____

A phrase is a group of words that has no finite verb (a verb with its subject). Some phrases do the work of an adverb. They tell *how, when* or *where* an action happens.

1. Choose the adverbial phrase that best completes each sentence.

> in the cage   after the film   during the afternoon
> with both hands   very quickly   at the school camp

a. The boys did their work _____ .

b. I made lots of new friends _____ .

c. I lifted the heavy box _____ .

d. We played cricket _____ .

e. The parrots are now back _____ .

f. I went to bed _____ .

2. Add an adverbial phrase of your own to complete each sentence.

a. The bird laid three eggs _____ .

b. The snake slithered _____ .

c. The lady had a ring _____ .

d. It was very hot _____ .

e. We walked down the street _____ .

f. You can stay up _____ .

Phrases

Name _____

Some phrases do the work of an adverb. They tell how, when or where an action happens.
We walked <u>into the classroom</u>.
Some phrases do the work of an adjective. They describe or add meaning to a noun.
The girl <u>with red hair</u> is my sister.
Some phrases do the work of a noun. They name something or answer the what? after the verb.
I have forgotten <u>the name of the boy</u>.

Look at each underlined phrase. Write whether it is doing the work of an adverb, adjective or noun.

a. He will be here <u>in a short time</u>.　　　　　_____

b. The boy <u>in a blue jumper</u> spoke to me.　　_____

c. I do not know <u>the name of the street</u>.　　　_____

d. Have you read <u>the latest book</u>?　　　　　_____

e. The man <u>with a grey beard</u> is my uncle.　　_____

f. I put the books <u>on the table</u>.　　　　　　_____

g. I saw Raj coming <u>along the road</u>.　　　　_____

h. I enjoy <u>eating hamburgers</u>.　　　　　　_____

i. The girl <u>in the blue swimming costume</u> is a champion.

_____

Clauses: Introduction and Answers

The distinction between clauses and phrases is that clauses always have a verb; the distinction between clauses and sentences is that clauses don't make complete sense on their own.

The following exercises use clauses to extend pupils' general grammatical awareness: pages 72 and 73 practise the idea of subordinate clauses, which add to the main clause of a sentence; pages 74 and 75 practise the terminology of subject and object, as first introduced under pronouns.

Answers to page 72

We picked the mushrooms/that were growing under the trees.

The police spoke to the man/who crashed his car.

We left the picnic/when it began to rain.

I asked the stranger/where he had come from.

Autumn is the season/when leaves change colour.

Bill ate tea/after he washed his hands.

Where is the book/I lent you last week?

The bus driver didn't know/which was my stop.

Answers to page 73

1a until		**1e** where	
1b because		**1f** whose	
1c who		All main clauses are first part of the sentence.	
1d that			

2 All main clauses are first part of the sentence.

Answers to page 74

	Subject	Verb
1a	The boy	hugged
1b	The black dog	won
1c	The game	is
1d	Mo	Did/win
1e	The girls	didn't enjoy
1f	The mouse	ran
1g	The blue car	won
1h	The stables	are

Answers to page 75

	Subject	Verb	Object
1a	The boy	hit	the dog
1b	Asha	Did/win	a prize
1c	The horse	jumped	the fence
1d	The teacher	praised	the small boy
1e	The savage dog	bit	the postman
1f	A tall boy	won	the race
1g	Dad	mopped	the floor

From Time-Savers for Teachers: Grammar Years 3-4. This page may be reproduced for classroom use.

71

Clauses

Name _____

A clause is a group of words that contains a verb and its subject. A main clause contains the main thought of the sentence and makes sense standing alone. A subordinate clause (dependent clause) does not make sense standing on its own. It adds information to the sentence.

1. Draw lines to match the main clauses to the correct subordinate clauses.

Main clause	**Subordinate clause**
We picked the mushrooms	when it began to rain.
The police spoke to the man	when leaves change colour.
We left the picnic	after he washed his hands.
I asked the stranger	that were growing under the trees.
Autumn is the season	who crashed his car.
Bill ate tea	where he had come from.
Where is the book	which was my stop.
The bus driver didn't know	I lent you last week?

2. Now choose two of the main clauses from question 1 and write new subordinate clauses to match. Write the sentences on the lines.

a. _____

_____

b. _____

_____

Clauses

A clause is a group of words that contains a verb and its subject. A main clause contains the main thought of the sentence and makes sense standing alone. A subordinate clause (dependent clause) does not make sense standing on its own. It adds information to the sentence.

1. Complete each sentence by adding a word from the box. Then circle the main clause in each sentence.

> who   because   that   where   whose   until

a. We must wait here _____ the rain stops.

b. Tom did not play _____ his foot was still sore.

c. I met the boy _____ won the race.

d. This is the dog _____ bit the postman.

e. We kept on walking _____ the snow was thick.

f. I spoke to the teacher _____ son is in our year.

2. Circle the main clauses. Underline the subordinate clauses.

a. John did not play because he had lost his boots.

b. Always look both ways before you cross a busy road.

c. Ravi cleaned his teeth after he had eaten his lunch.

d. We are not going to school today because it is a holiday.

e. We must leave after the first bell rings.

f. I cannot help you because I am too busy.

Clauses

Name _____

A clause is a group of words that contains a verb and its subject. The subject is the person or thing carrying out the action of the verb.

1. Underline the verb and circle the subject in the following main clauses.

a. The boy hugged the dog.

b. The black dog won the prize.

c. The game is over.

d. Did Mo win the race?

e. The girls didn't enjoy the lesson.

f. The mouse ran into the hole.

g. The blue car won the race.

h. The stables are out the back.

2. Now write three main clauses of your own. Make sure they have a verb and a subject.

a. _____

b. _____

c. _____

Clauses

A clause is a group of words that contains a verb and its subject. The subject is the person or thing carrying out the action of the verb. Some clauses also contain an object. The object is the person or thing that something is being done to.

1. Underline the verb and circle the subject in the following main clauses.
   Now draw a box around the object.

a. The boy hit the dog.

b. Did Asha win a prize?

c. The horse jumped the fence.

d. The teacher praised the small boy.

e. The savage dog bit the postman.

f. A tall boy won the race.

g. Mr Jones spoke to him.

h. Dad mopped the floor.

2. Now write three main clauses of your own. Make sure they have a verb, a subject and an object.

a. _____

b. _____

c. _____

Introduction to Punctuation

National Literacy Strategy objectives

Within the sections on Sentence construction, punctuation plays a crucial role in giving signposts to the meaning of the sentence:

Y3T2 S8: other uses of capitalisation from reading, e.g. names, headings, special emphasis, new lines in poetry;

Y4T2 S4: to recognise how commas, connectives and full stops are used to join and separate clauses; to identify in their writing where each is more effective;

Y3T3 W11: to use the apostrophe to spell further contracted forms, e.g. couldn't;

Y4T2 S2: to use the apostrophe accurately to mark possession;

Y3T1 S7: the basic conventions of speech punctuation through:

identifying speech marks in reading;

beginning to use in own writing;

using capital letters to mark the start of direct speech.

Introducing punctuation

As indicated above, this section builds on the use of capital letters and full stops, question marks or exclamation marks to demarcate the limits of sentences.

It extends the use of commas from lists to pauses in sentences.

It introduces the use of the apostrophe for contractions and for the possessive; as suggested in **Y4T2 S2**, these two uses need to be distinguished, if they are to be properly understood.

And finally models are given for the punctuation of speech in children's own writing.

Class activities

Begin reading a story to your class but do not pause at any punctuation marks. The children will be confused and will all object to the speed of your reading. Once this happens, lead them into a discussion about the need for punctuation marks, and the effects they have.

Make cards with large exclamation marks and question marks. Then read out words or short sentences and at the end of each one say, "Beep!". The children then hold up the card showing the punctuation mark they think is missing.

Worksheet answers

Answers are provided on pages 88 and 89.

Punctuation

Name _____

A capital letter is used for:
- **the first letter of a sentence.**
- **the first letter in names – books, plays, poems, films, songs, people, places, pets, days, months, countries, states, towns, mountains, rivers.**
- **the pronoun *I*.**

1. Rewrite the sentences using correct punctuation.

a. the cow drank the water in the tank

_____

b. i saw nicky yesterday

_____

c. last monday ned and freya went to a disco

_____

d. next september julie is going to live in manchester

_____

e. asha is in year three at the preston primary school

_____

2. Put a cross over the words that should not begin with a capital letter.

a. I know a tall Boy named John.
b. Asha has a Dog called Rover and a Cat called Cuddles.
c. There is a City called Manchester and a City called York.
d. Mr Smith has a Daughter called Ali.
e. The largest School in our Town is the Saint George's School.

Punctuation

Name _____

A capital letter is used for:
- **the first letter of a sentence.**
- **the first letter in names – books, plays, poems, films, songs, people, places, pets, days, months, countries, states, towns, mountains, rivers.**
- **the pronoun *I*.**

1. Complete each sentence in your own words. Make sure you use capital letters and full stops where they are needed.

a. My two best friends are _____

b. My birthday is in the month of _____

c. My teacher's name is _____

d. My favourite day of the week is _____

e. A large city in England is _____

f. Christmas is always in the month of _____

2. Rewrite the sentences using correct punctuation.

a. next saturday ling and peter are going to glasgow

_____

b. mike met mrs khan in spencer street

_____

c. the planet closest to pluto is neptune

_____

d. i read the book called plants of europe

_____

e. every easter and christmas we go on holiday to blackpool

_____

Punctuation

A statement sentence ends with a full stop.
A question sentence ends with a question mark.

In each line there are two sentences. Punctuate them correctly.

a. my brother's name is david have you met him

_____

_____

b. the largest city in scotland is glasgow have you been there

_____

_____

c. your dog rover is very large does he bark loudly

_____

_____

d. i read the book called big home have you read it

_____

_____

e. is that ian sitting over there why is he laughing

_____

_____

f. what is the tallest building in town is it the civic centre

_____

_____

g. what is this green vegetable is it spinach

_____

_____

h. why does a camel have a hump is it full of water

_____

_____

Punctuation

Name _____

An exclamation mark is used at the end of a sentence that expresses a strong emotion. Exclamation sentences are often short.

1. What might you call out if the following happened? Write an exclamation from the box.

> Ouch!   Look out!   How lovely!   Eek!   Yuk!

a. A ball you throw is heading towards a group of small children. _____

b. You sit on a prickle. _____

c. You find a big, black spider in your desk. _____

d. You eat something that tastes terrible. _____

e. You see a vase of beautiful flowers. _____

2. Add a full stop, question mark or exclamation mark at the end of each sentence. Hint: there are three of each.

a. Surprise

b. Southampton is a large city

c. Where is Paul going

d. Look out

e. What time is it

f. This book has lots of pages

g. I cut the lawn yesterday

h. When will you finish your lunch

i. That's amazing

Punctuation

Name _____

One of the uses of a comma is to separate words in lists. The commas replace the word 'and'.

1. Add commas where they are needed.

a. The names of three fruits are pears apples and bananas.

b. My best friends are Asha Michael and Julie.

c. My favourite pets are dogs cats goldfish and white mice.

d. The most popular sports in our school are cricket football golf and hockey.

e. Four things you can write with are pencils crayons pens and chalk.

f. The first four days of the week are Sunday Monday Tuesday and Wednesday.

2. Complete the sentences in your own words. Make sure you add commas where they are needed.

a. The names of four children in my class are _____

_____

b. Four months of the year are _____

_____

c. The names of four creatures that live in water are _____

_____

d. The names of four birds are _____

_____

e. The names of four farm animals are _____

_____

f. The names of four vegetables are _____

_____

Punctuation

Name _____

A contraction is a word made by joining two words together and leaving out some of the letters. An apostrophe is used to show where the letters have been left out.

1. Rewrite each sentence replacing the underlined words with a contraction from the box.

> I'll   it's   don't   can't   isn't

a. Nicky <u>is not</u> coming to my house now.

_____

b. Jo <u>can not</u> help you today.

_____

c. Wise people <u>do not</u> run across busy roads.

_____

d. I think <u>it is</u> going to rain this morning.

_____

e. <u>I will</u> make sure he gets there on time.

_____

2. Write the contraction of the underlined words.

a. Max <u>does not</u> like playing football. _____

b. The crow <u>could not</u> find the nest. _____

c. Catherine <u>was not</u> at the disco last night. _____

d. If she <u>does not</u> hurry <u>she will</u> be late. _____

Punctuation

Name _____

An apostrophe is used to show possession (that something belongs to something or someone). The possessive of a singular noun is formed by adding an *apostrophe* and *s* ('s) at the end of the word.

1. Rewrite each phrase using the possessive form of the noun. The first one has been done for you.

   a. the ears of the dog _____ the dog's ears _____

   b. the claws of the cat _____

   c. the rattle of the baby _____

   d. the car of the teacher _____

   e. the beak of the bird _____

2. Write an apostrophe where it is needed.

   a. My sisters toys are in the box.

   b. Kims mother will bring the pencils.

   c. The womans papers blew away.

   d. My fathers shoes are too big for me.

   e. The mans suitcases were heavy.

3. Write a sentence using the possessive of each noun.

   a. horse _____

   b. cow _____

   c. lady _____

   d. car _____

Punctuation

Name _____

An apostrophe is used to show possession (that something belongs to something or someone). The possessive of a plural noun is formed by:
- **adding an *apostrophe* if the word ends in 's' (horses' manes)**
- **or adding an *apostrophe s* ('s) if the word does not end in 's' (children's toys).**

1. Rewrite each phrase using the possessive form of the noun. The first one has been done for you.

a. the ears of the dogs_____ the dogs' ears _____

b. the toys of the babies _____

c. the food of the dogs _____

d. the engines of the cars _____

e. the hats of the children _____

2. Write an apostrophe where it is needed.

a. The childrens lunches are in the basket.

b. The horses tails were flicking.

c. The birds nests are empty.

d. The clowns noses were red.

e. The mens suitcases are heavy.

3. Write a sentence using the possessive of each noun.

a. cats_____

b. cows_____

c. womens_____

d. students_____

Punctuation

Direct speech is the exact words spoken by a person.
The words are usually enclosed in inverted commas.
"I am writing a story," said Meg.

Add the inverted commas where they are needed in these sentences.

a. I love cats, said Tom.

b. We are playing football today, yelled Mike.

c. Be careful. The teacher might catch you, whispered Joe.

d. What time will Sam arrive? asked Tom.

e. What a good idea! said the teacher.

f. Go! shouted the starter.

g. Fred yelled, Look out for the crazy horse!

h. The girl in the red dress said, I will help you lift that.

i. My best friend Tom said, Can you stay at my house for the weekend?

j. My mother said, I've told you before that you are not going to the party.

k. The man at the shop said, It costs five pounds.

l. I know it's hot, said the teacher, but please try to concentrate.

Punctuation

Name _____

Indirect speech reports a person's speech but does not necessarily quote the exact words used. The words are not enclosed in inverted commas.
Paul said that he was coming.

Change the direct speech into indirect speech. Remember, you don't need to use the exact words that the person said.

a. "What time is it?" asked Nancy.

_____

b. "It is going to be a lovely day," remarked Ling.

_____

c. "Where are you going?" asked Paul.

_____

d. "I've read that book before," moaned Tom.

_____

e. "I am going to win the race," boasted Mo.

_____

f. "Where will you get it from?" asked Sharm.

_____

g. Mum said, "It's too hot to go shopping."

_____

h. "We want more hamburgers!" yelled the boys.

_____

Answers to Punctuation

Answers to page 78

1a The cow drank the water in the tank.

1b I saw Nicky yesterday.

1c Last Monday, Ned and Freya went to a disco.

1d Next September, Julie is going to live in Manchester.

1e Asha is in Year Three at the Preston Primary School.

2a boy

2b dog cat

2c city city

2d daughter

2e school town

Answers to page 79

2a Next Saturday Ling and Peter are going to Glasgow.

2b Mike met Mrs Khan in Spencer Street.

2c The planet closest to Pluto is Neptune.

2d I read the book called Plants of Europe.

2e Every Easter and Christmas we go on holiday to Blackpool.

Answers to page 80

a My brother's name is David. Have you met him?

b The largest city in Scotland is Glasgow. Have you been there?

c Your dog Rover is very large. Does he bark loudly?

d I read the book called Big Home. Have you read it?

e Is that Raj sitting over there? Why is he laughing?

f What is the tallest building in town? Is it the Civic Centre?

g What is this green vegetable? Is it spinach?

h Why does a camel have a hump? Is it full of water?

Answers to page 81

1a Look out!

1b Ouch!

1c Eek!

1d Yuk!

1e How lovely!

2a !	**2f** .
2b .	**2g** .
2c ?	**2h** ?
2d !	**2i** !
2e ?	

Answers to page 82

1a pears, apples and bananas

1b Asha, Michael and Julie

1c dogs, cats, goldfish and white mice

1d cricket, football, golf and hockey

1e pencils, crayons, pens and chalk

1f Sunday, Monday, Tuesday and Wednesday

Answers to page 83

1a isn't

1b can't

1c don't

1d it's

1e I'll

2a doesn't

2b couldn't

2c wasn't

2d doesn't she'll

Answers to page 84

1b the cat's claws

1c the baby's rattle

1d the teacher's car

1e the bird's beak

2a My sister's toys

2b Kim's mother

2c The woman's papers

2d My father's shoes

2e The man's suitcases

Answers to page 85

1b the babies' toys

1c the dogs' food

1d the cars' engines

1e the children's hats

2a The children's lunches

2b The horses' tails

2c The birds' nests

2d The clowns' noses

2e The men's suitcases

Answers to page 86

a "I love cats," said Tom.

b "We are playing football today," yelled Mike.

c "Be careful. The teacher might catch you," whispered Joe.

d "What time will Sam arrive?" asked Tom.

e "What a good idea!" said the teacher.

f "Go!" shouted the starter.

g Fred yelled, "Look out for the crazy horse!"

h The girl in the red dress said, "I will help you lift that."

i My best friend Tom said, "Can you stay at my house for the weekend?"

j My mother said, "I've told you before that you are not going to the party."

k The man at the shop said, "It costs five pounds."

l "I know it's hot," said the teacher, "but please try to concentrate."

Answers to page 87

Suggested answers:

a Nancy asked what time it was.

b Ling remarked that it was going to be a lovely day.

c Paul asked where you were going.

d Tom moaned that he had read that book before.

e Mo boasted that he was going to win the race.

f Sharm asked where you would get it from.

g Mum said that it was too hot to go shopping.

h The boys yelled that they wanted more hamburgers.

89

Introduction to Vocabulary

National Literacy Strategy objectives

Although these exercises all link to objectives in the Word level section, they are essentially about grammatical use and constructions:

Y4T3 W11: to investigate compound words and recognise that they can aid spelling even where pronunciation obscures it, e.g. handbag, cupboard;

Y3T1 W11: to use their knowledge of prefixes to generate new words from root words, especially antonyms, happy/unhappy, appear/disappear;

Y3T1 W17: to generate synonyms for high frequency words, e.g. big, little, like, good, nice, nasty;

Y4T1 W6: to distinguish between the spelling and meanings of common homophones, e.g. to/two/too; they're/their/there; piece/peace.

Introducing vocabulary extension

These examples should occur and recur in teaching throughout Key Stage 2, as the need arises.

Many of the extensions depend on the concept of a root word, from which prefixes and suffixes may be added, to build new words with different meanings.

There is a danger that teaching homophones may actually increase confusion, but teachers should introduce each one at a point when they feel pupils would benefit from confronting their difficulty and realising that the different spellings derive logically from different grammatical origins.

Vocabulary

Name _____

A root word is a word from which other words are built.
A prefix is a group of letters placed at the beginning of a word.
A suffix is a group of letters added to the end of a word.

1. Write the root word.

a. indoors _____

b. unwashed _____

c. disagreement _____

d. awaken _____

e. unfinished _____

f. enjoyable _____

2. Rearrange the order of the prefix, root word and suffix to make the word.

a. bolt un ed (not locked) _____

b. appear dis ed (to go out of sight) _____

c. phone tele d (rang up) _____

d. ful truth un (telling lies) _____

e. ed un claim (not claimed) _____

f. ing re build (building again) _____

Vocabulary

Name _____

An antonym is a word that has the opposite meaning to another word.

1. Write the word from the box that has the opposite meaning to the underlined word.

> thin   cruel   dead   glad   sharp   shallow

a. We swam in the <u>deep</u> end of the pool. _____

b. I am <u>sorry</u> I was late. _____

c. This pig is very <u>fat</u>. _____

d. This knife is quite <u>blunt</u>. _____

e. I am sure it is <u>alive</u>. _____

f. Sam is very <u>kind</u> to animals. _____

2. Think of a word of your own that has the opposite meaning to the underlined word.

a. We began to walk <u>inside</u> the room. _____

b. The nuts on this wheel are quite <u>loose</u>. _____

c. This animal is <u>dangerous</u> to touch. _____

d. That line is <u>straight</u>. _____

e. This rock is <u>rough</u>. _____

f. Kylie got all her sums <u>right</u>. _____

Vocabulary

Name _____

A synonym is a word that has the same or similar meaning to another word.

1. Write the word from the box that has a similar meaning to the underlined word.

> truck   reply   pester   discovered   sound   certain

a. What was Mo's <u>answer</u>?   _____

b. A large <u>lorry</u> carried the furniture away.   _____

c. I am <u>sure</u> she will arrive on time.   _____

d. I heard a strange <u>noise</u>.   _____

e. What did he say when he <u>found</u> the money was missing?_____

f. Dad told me not to <u>annoy</u> him any longer.   _____

2. Think of synonyms of your own for each of the following words. Compare your answers with those of a friend.

a. cure _____

b. fix _____

c. clever _____

d. strange _____

e. present _____

f. tiny _____

Vocabulary

Name _____

A homophone is a word that sounds the same as another word but has a different meaning and different spelling.

1. Use a word from the box to complete each sentence.

> poor   wood   tail   hear   pour   would   tale   here

a. Our teacher told us a _____ about a dinosaur.

b. Did you _____ the roar of the lions at the zoo?

c. We cut some_____to make a campfire.

d. I asked Tom to _____the water in the bottle.

e. The dog spun around and tried to bite its own _____ .

f. I asked her to leave the books right_____.

g. He was too _____ to buy even a hamburger for lunch.

h. He said he _____ come if he was allowed to.

2. Circle the correct word in brackets.

a. It is rude to (**stair stare**) at people.

b. The old ship was (**towed toad**) out to sea and sunk.

c. Did you (**meet meat**) our new teacher?

d. I brushed the horse's (**main mane**).

e. This car is made of special (**steel steal**).

f. She was too (**week weak**) to leave hospital.

Answers to Vocabulary

Answers to page 91

1a door

1b wash

1c agree

1d wake

1e finish

1f joy

2a unbolted

2b disappeared

2c telephoned

2d untruthful

2e unclaimed

2f rebuilding

Answers to page 92

1a shallow

1b glad

1c thin

1d sharp

1e dead

1f cruel

Suggested answers:

2a outside

2b tight

2c safe

2d crooked

2e smooth

2f wrong

Answers to page 93

1a reply

1b truck

1c certain

1d sound

1e discovered

1f pester

Answers to page 94

1a tale

1b hear

1c wood

1d pour

1e tail

1f here

1g poor

1h would

2a stare

2b towed

2c meet

2d mane

2e steel

2f weak

Index